Preface

Welcome to the CTET PAPER I CLASS I TO V LANGUAGE 1 Book!

Teaching is a journey of learning, discovery, and personal growth. This book is designed to support you on that journey as you prepare for the Central Teacher Eligibility Test (CTET). Whether you are an aspiring educator or looking to enhance your knowledge, this book will equip you with essential concepts, strategies, and insights to excel in the exam and in your future teaching career.

Our goal is to make your learning experience meaningful and effective. Each chapter in this book has been carefully crafted to engage both your curiosity and critical thinking, covering core topics essential for the CTET exam. Along the way, you will find opportunities to reflect on best practices in education, the role of teachers in shaping society, and the importance of fostering an inclusive and supportive learning environment.

AF517049

Table of Contents

Chapter 1: Questions

1. What is the primary goal of reading unseen passages in language comprehension?

A) Memorization of facts

B) Understanding the structure of the text

C) Enhancing critical thinking skills

D) Testing writing ability

Answer: C

2. Which of the following best defines language pedagogy?

A) Study of syntax and semantics

B) The method and practice of teaching languages

C) Translation of literary works

D) Research in applied linguistics

Answer: B

3. What distinguishes acquisition from language learning?

A) Acquisition is intentional, learning is subconscious

B) Learning is formal, acquisition is subconscious

C) Acquisition requires classroom instruction

D) Learning only applies to native languages

Answer: B

4. Which principle emphasizes learning by doing in language teaching?

A) Structuralism

B) Behaviorism

C) Constructivism

D) Nativism

Answer: C

5. What is the most effective way to enhance listening skills in a language classroom?

A) Silent reading sessions

B) Speaking without listening

C) Exposure to audio resources

D) Memorizing vocabulary lists

Answer: C

6. Why is teaching language challenging in diverse classrooms?

A) Students have the same learning styles

B) All students are proficient in one language

C) Students come from different linguistic backgrounds

D) Teachers use uniform teaching techniques

Answer: C

7. Which of the following is not a language skill?

A) Listening

B) Writing

C) Memorizing

D) Speaking

Answer: C

8. How can teachers evaluate students' language proficiency?

A) Through aptitude tests only

B) By focusing solely on grammar

C) Using multiple assessment tools

D) Relying on peer feedback only

Answer: C

9. What type of material can be used for teaching spoken language?

A) Novels

B) Audio conversations

C) Charts and diagrams

D) Flashcards

Answer: B

10. What is the focus of remedial teaching in language learning?

A) Advancing the top learners

B) Addressing gaps in students' understanding

C) Preparing students for competitions

D) Teaching new languages

Answer: B

11. Which language teaching method emphasizes oral drills?

A) Grammar-Translation Method

B) Communicative Language Teaching

C) Audio-Lingual Method

D) Silent Way Method

Answer: C

12. Which type of comprehension is tested in a drama-based passage?

A) Technical language

B) Plot understanding

C) Philosophical interpretation

D) Literary theory

Answer: B

13. What is the primary focus of phonological awareness?

A) Syntax

B) Sounds in language

C) Reading comprehension

D) Writing skills

Answer: B

14. What role does peer interaction play in language learning?

A) Reduces learning opportunities

B) Promotes collaborative learning

C) Discourages independent thought

D) Makes language learning unnecessary

Answer: B

15. Which of the following methods is student-centered?

A) Lecture-based teaching

B) Communicative Language Teaching

C) Dictation-based learning

D) Grammar-Translation Method

Answer: B

16. What is the goal of using teaching aids in a language classroom?

A) To increase homework load

B) To support the learning process

C) To replace the teacher

D) To create confusion

Answer: B

17. What is an example of formative assessment?

A) Annual exams

B) Midterm exams

C) Daily quizzes

D) Final projects

Answer: C

18. Why is feedback important in language learning?

A) To punish mistakes

B) To encourage rote learning

C) To guide learners' improvement

D) To increase workload

Answer: C

19. Which of the following promotes autonomous learning?

A) Teacher-driven instruction

B) Group discussions

C) Assigning memorization tasks

D) Using self-study tools

Answer: D

20. How does reading poetry enhance language learning?

A) Increases factual knowledge

B) Builds appreciation for rhyme and rhythm

C) Focuses only on grammar rules

D) Limits vocabulary growth

Answer: B

21. Which strategy is suitable for vocabulary building?

A) Memorizing textbooks

B) Using flashcards

C) Listening to songs only

D) Ignoring new words

Answer: B

22. What is the function of a rubric in language evaluation?

A) To confuse students

B) To assign random grades

C) To provide clear assessment criteria

D) To skip assessments

Answer: C

23. Which approach integrates language skills with real-life contexts?

A) Grammar-Translation

B) Audio-Lingual

C) Task-Based Learning

D) Rote Memorization

Answer: C

24. How can technology support language learning?

A) By automating tests only

B) By offering digital textbooks exclusively

C) By providing interactive activities

D) By removing teacher involvement

Answer: C

25. What is the key to effective remedial teaching?

A) Treating all learners equally

B) Identifying individual learning needs

C) Avoiding extra resources

D) Assigning more homework

Answer: B

26. Which reading strategy involves scanning for specific information?

A) Skimming

B) Intensive reading

C) Extensive reading

D) Predicting

Answer: A

27. Why is scaffolding important in language teaching?

A) To give all answers to students

B) To build learning step-by-step

C) To ignore prior knowledge

D) To reduce student participation

Answer: B

28. Which aspect of language focuses on meaning?

A) Phonology

B) Syntax

C) Semantics

D) Phonetics

Answer: C

29. What is a graphic organizer used for in language learning?

A) To plan teaching schedules

B) To visualize relationships between ideas

C) To grade assignments

D) To track attendance

Answer: B

30. Which is an example of productive language skill?

A) Listening

B) Reading

C) Writing

D) Comprehending

Answer: C

31. What does the communicative approach emphasize?

A) Grammar rules

B) Communication and interaction

C) Translation accuracy

D) Memorization of dialogues

Answer: B

32. Which activity develops speaking skills effectively?

A) Silent reading

B) Group discussions

C) Grammar exercises

D) Watching videos passively

Answer: B

33. What is the purpose of using role-play in a language classroom?

A) To entertain students

B) To assess memorization

C) To practice real-life conversations

D) To avoid textbook content

Answer: C

34. How can a teacher manage language diversity in a classroom?

A) By using only one language for instruction

B) Ignoring students' backgrounds

C) Adopting multilingual strategies

D) Focusing on native speakers only

Answer: C

35. Which tool is most useful for evaluating listening skills?

A) Flashcards

B) Audio comprehension tests

C) Written assignments

D) Textbooks

Answer: B

36. What is an example of receptive language skills?

A) Speaking

B) Listening

C) Writing

D) Arguing

Answer: B

37. Which strategy helps learners improve reading fluency?

A) Reading aloud

B) Watching movies

C) Listening to music

D) Copying notes

Answer: A

38. What does differentiation in language teaching involve?

A) Giving identical assignments

B) Tailoring instruction to individual needs

C) Teaching only advanced learners

D) Eliminating assessments

Answer: B

39. Which component of language focuses on sentence structure?

A) Semantics

B) Syntax

C) Phonology

D) Morphology

Answer: B

40. What is the main goal of using language games in teaching?

A) To reduce academic pressure

B) To improve engagement and learning

C) To increase competition among students

D) To avoid lesson planning

Answer: B

41. Which teaching material is best suited for visual learners?

A) Audio recordings

B) Flashcards and charts

C) Worksheets

D) Group discussions

Answer: B

42. What is skimming in reading?

A) Reading quickly to get the main idea

B) Reading word-by-word for details

C) Avoiding complex texts

D) Memorizing passages

Answer: A

43. Why is context important in teaching vocabulary?

A) It discourages memorization

B) It makes learning meaningful

C) It complicates language learning

D) It limits word usage

Answer: B

44. Which teaching approach uses real-world tasks for learning?

A) Grammar-Translation

B) Task-Based Language Teaching

C) Silent Way

D) Structuralism

Answer: B

45. How does collaborative learning benefit students?

A) It promotes independent study

B) It discourages peer support

C) It encourages teamwork and communication

D) It focuses on individual grades

Answer: C

46. Which method improves pronunciation effectively?

A) Silent reading

B) Listening to native speakers

C) Writing essays

D) Grammar practice

Answer: B

47. What is code-switching?

A) Switching languages within a conversation

B) Learning to code in computer science

C) Changing seating arrangements

D) Skipping difficult lessons

Answer: A

48. Which type of reading emphasizes pleasure?

A) Intensive reading

B) Extensive reading

C) Critical reading

D) Close reading

Answer: B

49. What is the benefit of using realia in language teaching?

A) Reduces the need for preparation

B) Brings real-world objects into learning

C) Increases focus on theory

D) Limits classroom activities

Answer: B

50. What does scaffolding in teaching aim to achieve?

A) Eliminates student participation

B) Builds on prior knowledge gradually

C) Teaches only through lectures

D) Focuses on rote memorization

Answer: B

51. Which assessment type measures learning progress over time?

A) Diagnostic assessment

B) Summative assessment

C) Formative assessment

D) Aptitude assessment

Answer: C

52. Why is multicultural awareness important in language classrooms?

A) It discourages student participation

B) It promotes understanding among diverse learners

C) It focuses only on local cultures

D) It complicates lesson planning

Answer: B

53. What type of learner benefits most from kinesthetic activities?

A) Visual learners

B) Auditory learners

C) Tactile learners

D) Linguistic learners

Answer: C

54. What is the focus of phonics instruction?

A) Meaning of words

B) Relationship between sounds and letters

C) Sentence structure

D) Grammar rules

Answer: B

55. Which is an example of summative assessment?

A) Final exams

B) Classroom discussions

C) Daily participation

D) Practice quizzes

Answer: A

56. What role does storytelling play in language learning?

A) Discourages imagination

B) Improves comprehension and vocabulary

C) Increases rote learning

D) Limits student participation

Answer: B

57. What is the purpose of a portfolio in language assessment?

A) To collect random assignments

B) To showcase student progress and achievements

C) To replace all exams

D) To avoid feedback

Answer: B

58. Which language teaching approach focuses on natural communication?

A) Audio-Lingual Method

B) Communicative Language Teaching

C) Silent Way

D) Grammar-Translation

Answer: B

59. What does the term 'morphology' refer to in language studies?

A) Sound patterns

B) Sentence structure

C) Word formation

D) Text comprehension

Answer: C

60. Which strategy enhances listening comprehension?

A) Writing practice

B) Silent reading

C) Active listening tasks

D) Memorizing word lists

Answer: C

61. What is the primary focus of language immersion programs?

A) Teaching through translation

B) Providing instruction in the target language

C) Teaching grammar rules only

D) Limiting student interactions

Answer: B

62. What is the benefit of using group projects in language classes?

A) It eliminates individual accountability

B) It promotes teamwork and communication

C) It discourages active participation

D) It simplifies grading

Answer: B

63. What type of assessment provides immediate feedback?

A) Formative assessment

B) Summative assessment

C) Diagnostic assessment

D) Aptitude assessment

Answer: A

64. Which method helps improve writing skills?

A) Grammar memorization

B) Silent reading

C) Writing practice with feedback

D) Watching documentaries

Answer: C

65. What is a characteristic of learner-centered teaching?

A) Teacher lectures throughout

B) Students take ownership of learning

C) Assessments focus only on exams

D) Instruction follows strict schedules

Answer: B

66. Which element is essential for effective communication?

A) Memorizing vocabulary

B) Clear understanding of context

C) Reading silently

D) Avoiding interaction

Answer: B

67. What is the advantage of blended learning in language education?

A) It avoids the use of technology

B) It combines online and face-to-face learning

C) It limits classroom discussions

D) It reduces student engagement

Answer: B

68. Which activity is suitable for enhancing vocabulary retention?

A) Listening passively

B) Group games like word bingo

C) Writing essays without feedback

D) Ignoring new words

Answer: B

69. Why is student reflection important in language learning?

A) To reduce learning opportunities

B) To encourage self-assessment and improvement

C) To focus on teacher feedback only

D) To avoid mistakes

Answer: B

70. Which type of question promotes critical thinking in reading comprehension?

A) Multiple-choice questions

B) Yes/No questions

C) Open-ended questions

D) Matching questions

Answer: C

71. Which strategy promotes speaking fluency?

A) Listening silently

B) Role-playing real-life scenarios

C) Writing only essays

D) Avoiding conversations

Answer: B

72. What is the purpose of diagnostic assessment?

A) To grade final performance

B) To identify learning gaps early

C) To assign more homework

D) To compare students' abilities

Answer: B

73. What helps develop phonemic awareness?

A) Writing exercises

B) Identifying individual sounds in words

C) Memorizing grammar rules

D) Silent reading

Answer: B

74. Which material is most effective for teaching young learners?

A) Complex grammar books

B) Interactive storybooks

C) Academic journals

D) Dictionaries

Answer: B

75. What is the benefit of using multilingual resources in class?

A) It limits language exposure

B) It promotes linguistic diversity

C) It discourages native language use

D) It complicates learning

Answer: B

76. Which assessment technique measures real-time performance?

A) Portfolio assessment

B) Peer review

C) Oral presentations

D) Standardized tests

Answer: C

77. What is fluency in language learning?

A) Perfect grammar usage

B) Speed and ease in communication

C) Memorizing vocabulary lists

D) Reading without understanding

Answer: B

78. Which method emphasizes meaning over form?

A) Grammar-Translation Method

B) Silent Way

C) Communicative Approach

D) Direct Method

Answer: C

79. How can teachers foster a positive learning environment?

A) Discouraging mistakes

B) Encouraging exploration and participation

C) Limiting questions

D) Focusing only on grades

Answer: B

80. Which skill is essential for decoding words?

A) Syntax awareness

B) Phonics knowledge

C) Grammatical precision

D) Writing practice

Answer: B

81. Which teaching strategy supports active learning?

A) Lectures only

B) Group discussions

C) Passive listening

D) Memorization

Answer: B

82. What is the purpose of self-assessment in language learning?

A) To avoid teacher feedback

B) To reflect on personal progress

C) To replace all assessments

D) To discourage improvement

Answer: B

83. Which element is critical in developing reading comprehension?

A) Speed reading

B) Understanding text meaning

C) Ignoring unfamiliar words

D) Avoiding discussion

Answer: B

84. What is peer assessment?

A) Grading each other's work

B) Ignoring classmates' progress

C) Memorizing peers' essays

D) Avoiding collaborative learning

Answer: A

85. Which activity builds listening skills?

A) Listening to podcasts

B) Writing without feedback

C) Reading silently

D) Memorizing vocabulary

Answer: A

86. Which technique helps students grasp sentence structure?

A) Diagramming sentences

B) Watching TV shows

C) Memorizing definitions

D) Avoiding complex texts

Answer: A

87. What role do open-ended questions play in learning?

A) They limit student creativity

B) They encourage critical thinking

C) They promote rote memorization

D) They focus only on factual recall

Answer: B

88. Why is storytelling effective for language development?

A) It restricts vocabulary usage

B) It makes learning engaging and memorable

C) It reduces imagination

D) It replaces all assessments

Answer: B

89. Which reading strategy involves predicting content?

A) Skimming

B) Previewing

C) Scanning

D) Memorizing

Answer: B

90. What is the role of feedback in formative assessment?

A) To criticize students

B) To guide learning improvement

C) To finalize grades

D) To discourage students

Answer: B

91. Which strategy helps students retain new vocabulary?

A) Flashcard practice

B) Avoiding repetition

C) Ignoring unknown words

D) Memorizing all textbooks

Answer: A

92. How can teachers support diverse learners in language classrooms?

A) Using one teaching strategy for all

B) Adapting methods to different needs

C) Ignoring individual differences

D) Teaching only native speakers

Answer: B

93. What is the aim of task-based learning?

A) To complete isolated drills

B) To practice language through meaningful tasks

C) To memorize rules

D) To avoid collaboration

Answer: B

94. Which tool measures students' progress over time?

A) Homework assignments

B) Portfolios

C) Attendance records

D) Peer assessments

Answer: B

95. How can teachers make learning more student-centered?

A) By delivering long lectures

B) By promoting active participation

C) By avoiding discussions

D) By focusing on grades only

Answer: B

96. What is the purpose of remedial classes?

A) To teach advanced topics

B) To address students' learning difficulties

C) To reduce study hours

D) To eliminate assessments

Answer: B

97. Which reading strategy is used to locate specific details quickly?

A) Scanning

B) Extensive reading

C) Critical reading

D) Intensive reading

Answer: A

98. Which activity is most effective for developing writing skills?

A) Writing with peer feedback

B) Reading novels silently

C) Watching TV

D) Memorizing essays

Answer: A

99. What is meant by receptive skills?

A) Skills involving language production

B) Skills involving comprehension

C) Memorization-based skills

D) Only speaking skills

Answer: B

100. Which tool promotes collaborative learning?

A) Flashcards

B) Group projects

C) Lectures

D) Silent reading

Answer: B

Chapter 2: Questions

101. What is a common challenge in teaching language in diverse classrooms?

A) Uniform learning pace among students

B) Differences in students' language backgrounds

C) All students speaking the same language

D) Lack of teaching materials

Answer: B

102. What is a key principle of communicative language teaching?

A) Memorizing vocabulary lists

B) Practicing communication in meaningful contexts

C) Focusing solely on grammar

D) Avoiding interaction

Answer: B

103. Which strategy promotes active listening?

A) Taking notes during lectures

B) Ignoring unfamiliar words

C) Practicing passive reading

D) Listening without engagement

Answer: A

104. What is one benefit of role-playing in language learning?

A) Avoids textbook content

B) Encourages real-life communication practice

C) Focuses only on written skills

D) Limits student participation

Answer: B

105. Which tool helps assess oral proficiency?

A) Standardized written tests

B) Audio recordings of student speech

C) Silent quizzes

D) Reading comprehension tests

Answer: B

106. How can teachers support students struggling with reading comprehension?

A) By skipping complex texts

B) By teaching decoding strategies

C) By focusing only on spoken language

D) By avoiding reading assignments

Answer: B

107. Which activity enhances pronunciation?

A) Writing practice

B) Reading aloud

C) Memorizing grammar rules

D) Watching videos silently

Answer: B

108. What is the main goal of extensive reading?

A) Reading quickly without understanding

B) Reading for pleasure and exposure to language

C) Memorizing every sentence

D) Avoiding discussions

Answer: B

109. Which material is most suitable for beginner learners?

A) Complex academic texts

B) Illustrated storybooks

C) Research articles

D) Literary criticism

Answer: B

110. Which language skill involves both comprehension and production?

A) Speaking

B) Listening

C) Reading

D) Writing

Answer: A

111. How does feedback improve writing skills?

A) By pointing out mistakes only

B) By encouraging students to reflect and revise

C) By reducing writing opportunities

D) By limiting creativity

Answer: B

112. Which assessment method provides detailed feedback?

A) Multiple-choice tests

B) Formative assessment

C) Summative assessment

D) Standardized exams

Answer: B

113. What is a challenge of online language learning?

A) Increased student interaction

B) Difficulty in assessing speaking skills

C) Access to unlimited resources

D) Opportunities for collaborative learning

Answer: B

114. Which practice develops both listening and speaking skills?

A) Reading silently

B) Participating in debates

C) Memorizing vocabulary

D) Watching TV without interaction

Answer: B

115. Which teaching method involves learning through projects?

A) Audio-Lingual Method

B) Grammar-Translation Method

C) Project-Based Learning

D) Silent Way

Answer: C

116. What is a benefit of peer learning?

A) Limits collaborative efforts

B) Promotes mutual learning and support

C) Discourages independent work

D) Focuses on individual achievements

Answer: B

117. What does phonemic awareness involve?

A) Memorizing word meanings

B) Identifying sounds in spoken words

C) Writing complex essays

D) Reading silently

Answer: B

118. How can teachers encourage self-directed learning?

A) By giving students control over tasks

B) By providing strict instructions

C) By eliminating assessments

D) By limiting learning materials

Answer: A

119. What is the purpose of formative assessment?

A) To evaluate students at the end of a term

B) To monitor ongoing learning progress

C) To assign final grades

D) To prepare for competitions

Answer: B

120. Which tool enhances visual learners' engagement?

A) Podcasts

B) Graphic organizers

C) Audio books

D) Grammar handouts

Answer: B

121. How can teachers assess students' listening skills effectively?

A) By giving written tests

B) By conducting listening activities

C) By assigning reading assignments

D) By avoiding audio materials

Answer: B

122. What is scaffolding in education?

A) Teaching all concepts at once

B) Providing temporary support to learners

C) Reducing student participation

D) Limiting classroom activities

Answer: B

123. What is a primary feature of student-centered learning?

A) Teachers control all activities

B) Students actively participate and take ownership

C) Learning is teacher-driven

D) Strict adherence to schedules

Answer: B

124. What is the purpose of reading aloud in class?

A) To improve grammar skills

B) To enhance pronunciation and fluency

C) To avoid comprehension tasks

D) To limit speaking practice

Answer: B

125. Which strategy is most effective for vocabulary retention?

A) Rote memorization

B) Repetition through games

C) Skipping unknown words

D) Ignoring word meaning

Answer: B

126. What is a characteristic of a reflective learner?

A) Avoids feedback

B) Engages in self-assessment

C) Memorizes without understanding

D) Depends only on teacher input

Answer: B

127. What is the focus of summative assessment?

A) Ongoing feedback

B) Evaluating final achievement

C) Monitoring daily progress

D) Identifying early challenges

Answer: B

128. Which strategy enhances reading comprehension?

A) Scanning for keywords

B) Predicting and questioning

C) Memorizing complex texts

D) Avoiding discussions

Answer: B

129. What is one benefit of remedial teaching?

A) Helps advanced learners only

B) Addresses specific learning gaps

C) Eliminates the need for assessments

D) Focuses on group projects only

Answer: B

130. How can technology support language learning?

A) By replacing teachers

B) Through interactive applications

C) By limiting student engagement

D) By discouraging collaboration

Answer: B

131. Which tool is useful for peer feedback?

A) Flashcards

B) Rubrics

C) Multiple-choice tests

D) Silent assessments

Answer: B

132. How can teachers build students' confidence in speaking?

A) By discouraging participation

B) By providing a supportive environment

C) By focusing only on writing skills

D) By avoiding oral assessments

Answer: B

133. What does metacognition involve?

A) Memorizing definitions

B) Thinking about one's thinking process

C) Avoiding critical reflection

D) Skipping assessments

Answer: B

134. Which method fosters collaborative learning?

A) Group projects

B) Silent reading

C) Individual essays

D) Grammar translation

Answer: A

135. What is a benefit of using rubrics?

A) Limits grading criteria

B) Provides clear performance expectations

C) Focuses only on final exams

D) Reduces feedback opportunities

Answer: B

136. Which activity develops critical thinking?

A) Memorizing facts

B) Open-ended discussions

C) Copying notes

D) Avoiding group tasks

Answer: B

137. Which assessment tool measures individual progress over time?

A) Portfolio

B) Midterm exams

C) Final assessments

D) Peer feedback

Answer: A

138. How does storytelling engage learners?

A) Limits creativity

B) Connects language with emotions

C) Reduces vocabulary

D) Replaces classroom activities

Answer: B

139. Which strategy improves listening skills?

A) Listening to music actively

B) Ignoring audio resources

C) Writing without feedback

D) Watching TV without focus

Answer: A

140. What is one challenge in evaluating oral language skills?

A) Easy grading

B) Subjectivity in assessment

C) Lack of participation

D) Over-reliance on exams

Answer: B

141. Which method integrates language with content learning?

A) Content and Language Integrated Learning (CLIL)

B) Grammar-Translation Method

C) Audio-Lingual Method

D) Direct Method

Answer: A

142. How can teachers use multimedia effectively in language classrooms?

A) Only for entertainment purposes

B) To provide audio-visual context for learning

C) To replace class participation

D) To eliminate textbook use

Answer: B

143. What is the purpose of interactive reading sessions?

A) To test memory only

B) To engage students with the text actively

C) To focus only on pronunciation

D) To discourage group discussions

Answer: B

144. How can teachers foster metacognitive skills in students?

A) By giving fixed instructions

B) By encouraging reflection on learning strategies

C) By avoiding discussions on thinking

D) By focusing only on test results

Answer: B

145. What is the benefit of using songs in language learning?

A) Enhances memorisation without understanding

B) Makes vocabulary learning enjoyable

C) Discourages critical thinking

D) Avoids grammar practice

Answer: B

146. Which activity helps develop narrative skills?

A) Retelling stories

B) Writing definitions

C) Memorizing grammar rules

D) Watching videos silently

Answer: A

147. What is a common feature of blended learning?

A) Combining online and in-person instruction

B) Focusing only on face-to-face learning

C) Avoiding technology use

D) Replacing teacher interaction

Answer: A

148. Which tool measures listening comprehension accurately?

A) Written essays

B) Audio-based tests

C) Silent readings

D) Vocabulary quizzes

Answer: B

149. What is the primary focus of communicative competence?

A) Using language in real-world contexts

B) Memorizing grammar rules

C) Writing formal essays

D) Avoiding conversations

Answer: A

150. Which strategy enhances peer learning?

A) Group activities and discussions

B) Assigning individual work only

C) Reducing interaction

D) Memorizing independently

Answer: A

151. What is the advantage of task-based learning?

A) Encourages meaningful language use

B) Focuses only on memorisation

C) Avoids real-world application

D) Reduces active participation

Answer: A

152. How can storytelling improve vocabulary acquisition?

A) Limits word exposure

B) Provides context for new words

C) Focuses only on syntax

D) Replaces grammar practice

Answer: B

153. Which assessment focuses on end-of-term learning?

A) Summative assessment

B) Formative assessment

C) Diagnostic assessment

D) Peer assessment

Answer: A

154. Which strategy promotes learner autonomy?

A) Teacher-centered instruction

B) Assigning self-directed tasks

C) Memorization-only approach

D) Limiting independent activities

Answer: B

155. Which material is ideal for teaching young learners?

A) Illustrated storybooks

B) Academic journals

C) Research papers

D) Grammar textbooks

Answer: A

156. Which activity helps build confidence in speaking?

A) Debates and discussions

B) Silent writing exercises

C) Memorizing word lists

D) Avoiding group activities

Answer: A

157. What does formative assessment provide?

A) Final grades

B) Ongoing feedback for improvement

C) Certification

D) Competition results

Answer: B

158. Which approach focuses on using language naturally?

A) Communicative Language Teaching

B) Grammar-Translation Method

C) Silent Way

D) Audio-Lingual Method

Answer: A

159. How can teachers encourage reflective learning?

A) By assigning self-assessment tasks

B) By focusing only on grades

C) By discouraging feedback

D) By avoiding goal setting

Answer: A

160. Which tool measures reading comprehension?

A) Multiple-choice questions

B) Vocabulary quizzes

C) Oral presentations

D) Audio tests

Answer: A

161. What does phonics instruction focus on?

A) Letters and sounds

B) Word meanings

C) Sentence structure

D) Memorizing grammar rules

Answer: A

162. How can teachers manage diverse classrooms?

A) Using a one-size-fits-all approach

B) Adapting instruction to learners' needs

C) Ignoring student backgrounds

D) Reducing participation

Answer: B

163. Which method promotes fluency?

A) Silent reading

B) Conversations and role-plays

C) Memorizing grammar rules

D) Writing definitions

Answer: B

164. What is the benefit of using portfolios?

A) Avoids assessments

B) Shows students' learning journey

C) Replaces teacher feedback

D) Focuses only on test scores

Answer: B

165. How can teachers make assessments fair?

A) By providing rubrics

B) By grading subjectively

C) By avoiding feedback

D) By limiting evaluation tools

Answer: A

166. Which method uses real-world tasks?

A) Task-Based Learning

B) Silent Way

C) Grammar-Translation

D) Rote Memorization

Answer: A

167. What role do visuals play in language learning?

A) Complicate lessons

B) Enhance comprehension

C) Reduce participation

D) Replace written material

Answer: B

168. What is an example of receptive skill?

A) Writing essays

B) Listening to podcasts

C) Speaking to peers

D) Engaging in debates

Answer: B

169. How can teachers foster critical thinking?

A) By giving open-ended questions

B) By assigning rote tasks

C) By avoiding discussions

D) By focusing on grammar only

Answer: A

170. What is an example of productive skill?

A) Speaking in class

B) Listening to lectures

C) Reading silently

D) Watching videos

Answer: A

171. Which activity supports listening development?

A) Group conversations

B) Writing essays

C) Memorizing definitions

D) Copying notes

Answer: A

172. What is the role of feedback in learning?

A) To punish students

B) To guide improvement

C) To limit participation

D) To avoid assessments

Answer: B

173. How can storytelling enhance listening skills?

A) By increasing passive learning

B) By engaging students emotionally

C) By avoiding new words

D) By focusing only on written language

Answer: B

174. Which tool is used to track learning progress?

A) Portfolio

B) Flashcards

C) Attendance sheet

D) Grammar workbook

Answer: A

175. What promotes effective communication?

A) Clear and meaningful interaction

B) Memorizing texts

C) Avoiding speaking

D) Focusing on written tests only

Answer: A

176. What helps develop reading fluency?

A) Reading aloud regularly

B) Memorizing sentences

C) Avoiding complex texts

D) Skipping unfamiliar words

Answer: A

177. What is the goal of formative feedback?

A) Assign grades

B) Support continuous improvement

C) Replace assessments

D) Avoid mistakes

Answer: B

178. What supports self-assessment?

A) Peer evaluation

B) Reflection journals

C) Summative exams

D) Multiple-choice quizzes

Answer: B

179. Which tool evaluates oral proficiency?

A) Audio tests

B) Portfolios

C) Vocabulary quizzes

D) Flashcards

Answer: A

180. Which method promotes natural conversation?

A) Communicative Language Teaching

B) Grammar drills

C) Memorizing dialogues

D) Silent practice

Answer: A

181. What does student-centred learning emphasise?

A) Teacher-led activities

B) Student autonomy and involvement

C) Memorizing content

D) Avoiding discussions

Answer: B

182. What develops writing skills effectively?

A) Writing practice with feedback

B) Copying notes

C) Avoiding revisions

D) Memorizing grammar rules

Answer: A

183. What is the purpose of diagnostic tests?

A) Identify learning challenges

B) Assign final grades

C) Replace assessments

D) Test only advanced learners

Answer: A

184. What enhances vocabulary retention?

A) Repetition and context usage

B) Avoiding new words

C) Memorizing without meaning

D) Skipping practice

Answer: A

185. How can teachers encourage participation?

A) By creating a supportive environment

B) By discouraging questions

C) By focusing only on grades

D) By limiting discussions

Answer: A

186. Which strategy helps build reading comprehension?

A) Predicting and questioning

B) Avoiding complex texts

C) Focusing only on speed

D) Skipping unfamiliar words

Answer: A

187. What makes listening challenging?

A) Fast speech and unfamiliar accents

B) Clear pronunciation

C) Slow conversations

D) Repetitive sentences

Answer: A

188. Which tool helps assess students' vocabulary knowledge?

A) Multiple-choice tests

B) Listening exercises

C) Role-play activities

D) Group discussions

Answer: A

189. What is an essential element in teaching pronunciation?

A) Listening to native speakers

B) Memorizing grammar rules

C) Writing long essays

D) Avoiding oral practice

Answer: A

190. Which method encourages students to learn by doing?

A) Experiential learning

B) Grammar-Translation Method

C) Silent reading

D) Memorization drills

Answer: A

191. What type of questions promote creative thinking?

A) Open-ended questions

B) Yes/No questions

C) True/False questions

D) Multiple-choice questions

Answer: A

192. How can teachers create an inclusive classroom environment?

A) By addressing students' individual needs

B) By following the same teaching style for all

C) By limiting participation

D) By focusing only on grades

Answer: A

193. What is the goal of using authentic materials in language teaching?

A) To expose students to real-world language

B) To make learning more difficult

C) To avoid structured lessons

D) To replace grammar lessons

Answer: A

194. Which activity promotes fluency in speaking?

A) Role-plays and simulations

B) Memorizing vocabulary lists

C) Copying notes from the board

D) Writing essays silently

Answer: A

195. What is a key characteristic of formative assessment?

A) Provides immediate feedback for improvement

B) Focuses only on final exams

C) Limits student-teacher interaction

D) Assigns final grades

Answer: A

196. Which strategy supports differentiated instruction?

A) Providing varied tasks based on students' needs

B) Using identical materials for all learners

C) Reducing learning opportunities

D) Assigning the same homework to everyone

Answer: A

197. How can teachers support students' speaking skills?

A) By encouraging participation in discussions

B) By focusing only on written assignments

C) By avoiding oral tasks

D) By grading participation harshly

Answer: A

198. Which assessment tool evaluates both speaking and listening?

A) Oral presentations

B) Vocabulary quizzes

C) Writing exercises

D) Reading comprehension tests

Answer: A

199. What is an example of authentic language use?

A) Ordering food in a restaurant

B) Memorizing word lists

C) Writing grammar rules

D) Copying textbook sentences

Answer: A

200. Which approach enhances students' intrinsic motivation?

A) Assigning meaningful, real-world tasks

B) Using fear of failure

C) Focusing only on grades

D) Giving repetitive drills

Answer: A

© Author and Publisher 2024

9 789349 018648

Printed at Repro India Ltd.